LIFE OF ABUNDANCE

How To Live a Life of Abundance

by

NICHOLAS WOODRUFF

Dedication

This book is dedicated to God first and foremost because nothing in the universe is possible without His infinite energy and wisdom. To my family, especially my two wonderful sons, Nicholas and Braylen, who I have dedicated my life to. To my mother, who stayed supporting me through all my trials and tribulations. To my father, who gave me street smarts, and to my stepfather. To my brother and sister, Tomeka and Karl, who were always there when I needed them as a child. My friends who I hold close to my heart. The mothers of my children because without them, I wouldn't have been blessed with my two sons. All the people that had an impact in my life, all of which were positive encounters, even if a few were initially seen as negative.

Table of Contents

INTRODUCTION

⌒

Welcome to your introduction to the first day of the rest of your life.

Life is not what you think. The truth about wealth and prosperity is different from what you previously were taught. You may think that prosperity and wealth are ultimately centered on having money or material things. Some think of a life of abundance as money, fancy cars, and jewelry. Some men may think a beautiful woman may also be a sign of prosperity. I won't say this is not true, but this is only the beginning.

Growing up in Detroit, Michigan, I've seen many things. My life started in one of the poorest sections in the city. As I grew older, my family began to acquire a little more money. We have never been financially wealthy, but we were better off than others with whom I went to school. I have seen a lot in my short time on this planet. I've been poor, and I've had a life of abundance. I cannot say I've been truly wealthy as far as money goes, but that is what this book is about. This book is about the true meaning of wealth. Many people will say, "well, it's only money." But we have all seen and heard the stories of people with money. Their life is no better than a person working a regular 9 to 5. The media and television will tell you otherwise, but you can see the truth in their eyes. They have problems just like you and me. They have faced health scares, death in their families, and even financial troubles. But when a person is living a true life of abundance, none of these things matter because they are truly wealthy and understand the real meaning of life. In my opinion, the true meaning of life is a life of abundance. This book will discuss the true meaning of life and how to live a life of abundance. No education is required for this. However, education will greatly escalate some of the categories you wish to achieve the life you desire.

During my years as a social worker, I have come across different types of people. Most of them were financially unstable and did not have much money. But for some reason, I came to realize that a lot of them had more than me, even though I had a good job. When it was time to talk with them about their issues and need for assistance, some of them were out of town on summer vacation or just seemed to be in a very happy place mentally. Of course, some may have had illnesses that would prevent them from such activities, but that's a whole different scenario.

Let's play around a bit. Let's say, for example, that you have a nicely seasoned steak. It's been cooked to your liking. This should be the best steak you've ever had in your life. You have been waiting for this and are salivating over it. You worked hard to prepare the steak as you thought you would have liked it. You take a bite. It is absolutely delicious. But something is missing. You take another bite. You realize that it is missing a lot of key elements that would allow you to properly enjoy this steak. You worked hard for this steak, but because you concentrated only on the meat portion of the meal, you forgot that you need sides, seasonings, and maybe a glass of wine to make it a full meal. This is the beginning of how those who have acquired a fortune start to realize how money isn't the end-all. I've seen those who have worked their whole lives for fortune only to realize once they have achieved their dream bank account number, they have forgotten the other key ingredients for a life of abundance. In this book, we will break them down for you. After reading this book, you will be further on your way for a life of abundance than you have ever been before. Some may finally realize that they have a life of abundance and not even know it.

Unfortunately, you have been brainwashed to think that abundance and prosperity center around money for those of you who have a life of abundance and do not even know it. So, because you may not have all the money in the world, you have totally missed the other things that account for prosperity. You've been watching TV, social media, reality shows, and now your mind thinks that the things that you see in the media are what make up a happy life.

The benefit of this book is that it will help you realize that you may be wealthier than you knew. And if you are not, a simple change of mindset will change your life for the better. You may already know about these things, but you may not have realized how important they are to concentrate on, show gratitude for, and work on in your everyday life. If you have children, these things are something great to teach your children early, especially in a world of visual stimulation. They need sustenance and to understand that they need more than material things to be happy.

True wealth is acquired when you have things that money *can* buy, but most importantly, what money *can't* buy. Technically, an infinite number of things make up a truly wealthy life. However, in this book, we will discuss some of the main components of what I believe make up a life of abundance.

CHAPTER ONE

⌒

Health

When it comes to wealth, your mind and body are your most valuable assets. And when it comes to being healthy, a good diet is key. Some would say that a person isn't completely wealthy without a healthy body and mind.

Diet is the most important thing that you must get a handle on to acquire good health. Sure, some factors are out of our control when it comes to being healthy. In my opinion, they are minuscule when it comes to the benefits of a good diet. I won't spend a lot of time mentioning the things we can't control. This book is intended to focus on the positive things that you will be able to change in your life.

We will start with water. Water is the most important thing you will ever put in your body. It is your life force. It is your cleanser. By drinking more water, you can decrease the number of illnesses your body has. Let's start by talking about blood pressure. High blood pressure is caused primarily by a poor diet. Sure, genetics play a part, but those genetically predisposed to hypertension need to pay close attention to how much water they drink, starting before there are symptoms. The cause of high blood pressure is mostly salt or sodium and lack of exercise. You can say that people become allergic to sodium as they get older, which causes high blood pressure or hypertension. They must watch the amount of salt they ingest. To counteract the amount of sodium they take in, they must drink close to a gallon of water a day to flush the sodium out. It sounds like a lot, but when you have the "*time,*" which we will talk about later, it's no big deal because you have set aside extra time to take care of yourself. Because your body is your most precious, expensive, and costly possession, you should drink a glass of water an hour until you have reached your goal. And by water, I mean actual water. Soda, fruit juice, or water with added ingredients do not count. Because your body gathers all the toxins and sodium in your body, flushing it out of your system, you may go to the restroom more. Think of it as every time you go to the bathroom, you are one step closer to acquiring good health, which ultimately gets you one step closer to your true goal of a life of abundance.

Eating a healthy diet will ultimately bring you closer to your goals. Eating a balanced diet seems like something that everyone should already know is important. But it must not be as important to people as it should be, as you can tell by the number of pharmacies on every corner. Once again, of course, some ailments are inevitable, but a lot are avoidable. By doing daily exercises, staying away from fried foods, and eating more fruits and vegetables, you will keep your body healthy and help your it run more smoothly. Also, keeping tabs on your fiber intake to keep everything flowing correctly is essential, versus staying in your body too long and eventually turning toxic. To tie these things together, the healthier you choose to live, the easier it will be to keep your mind sharp. A sharp mind will ensure you are ready to accept the gifts that the universe has to offer you.

Men and women may experience hormonal changes with a lackluster diet. And by hormones, we are talking more than just testosterone and/ or estrogen. The body produces about 50 different hormones, all of which have different purposes. It is imperative to feed your body the necessary nourishment and nutrients needed to perform properly. If the body cannot regulate the hormones it produces to keep the body performing at its optimum capability, a person will experience side effects. Without the proper regulation of hormones, a person may experience mood swings and poor brain function. These issues can affect your ability to live your best life and acquire a life full of abundance.

Treat your body like a new car. You know how you feel when you just get a car. The difference between your body and a new car is you can get a new car, but not a new body.

Low-quality meats and processed foods poison your bloodstream little by little. Long exposure to processed foods, especially meats, can cause cancer. And even if it doesn't cause an apparent illness, eating these foods dulls your sharp mind, making it harder to concentrate or keep a stable emotional state. This makes it more difficult to reach your goals and will ultimately slow your progress of living a life of abundance.

Some substances make it harder to keep your body from performing at its optimum ability. Alcohol is one of those. Keep in mind that alcohol is nothing but putting toxins in your body. The toxins give the body and mind the resultant feeling that comes with taking alcohol. The alcohol poisons your body slightly. Eating an unhealthy diet is the same thing. However, unlike alcohol, it takes a lot longer than 24 hours to get bad food choices out of your mind, body, and even spirit.

Drugs and alcohol. Nowadays, it seems like everyone drinks, and if they are not drinking, they are smoking marijuana or cigarettes. Liquor stores are on just about every corner in some neighborhoods. We are also starting to see marijuana stores pop up all over my town. These things are so readily available, it almost seems like there is nothing wrong with drinking and smoking daily. I'm not here to judge anyone, but I will say this: From my own personal experience in my life, and as a social worker, the one who smokes and drinks the most loses. I've seen many lives lost to the bottle and a lot of time wasted from the excess of weed.

Drugs and alcohol are bad for you. Sure, it's okay to have a small drink occasionally. But for some of us, just like eating too much, it's very easy to drink too much. And just like we eat the wrong things, we drink the wrong things. How can one be totally in tune with the almighty universe if he has alcohol and marijuana pollutants in his bloodstream? Both alcohol and marijuana may be beneficial in very, very small doses, but it's easy to abuse them. Drug and alcohol abuse distorts your view of the world, harms your body, and could possibly harm others. We all know someone has been injured in a drunk driving accident. Or the guy from the neighborhood who smokes weed all the time and does nothing with his life. If you don't know any of these people, then look in the mirror and you will probably see the person standing in front of you. My advice is to leave these things totally alone. The reason I say totally is that most people don't have the ability to do things sparingly. Sparingly means once, maybe twice a week. I had to look in the mirror, do a reality check, and tell myself that I was spending money on alcohol and weed, which took me off course from my life of abundance. By doing this, I actually had more money because I wasn't spending it on things that altered my mind and spirit, which also led me to spend money on other foolish things that the media has marketed to those who live that type of lifestyle. So, in short, when I cut the smoking and drinking out completely, I was able to see the gifts that the universe had already given me, plus the gifts that had been on the other side of the lackluster lifestyle I was living. Quitting substances that had no true value in my life gave me a pay increase in multiple ways. I freed up thousands of dollars a year since I stopped, plus stopping the useless substances gave me a clearer picture of my goals and garnered pay increases because I was able to focus on the things I needed to focus on. And last but not least, I was able to come up with the idea to write this book.

Drinking and smoking cause health problems. I won't go through the normal heart and lung aspect because I'm sure you've heard that before. I'll try a different angle. For men, drinking and smoking in excess can lead to hormonal issues. That means that excessive drinking and/or excessive smoking that is used to relax and get us in the mood eventually catches up to your body, making it difficult to please the opposite sex, whether physically or mentally. Now I can't speak for everyone, but things of that nature are what living a life of abundance is about. It's one of life's most enjoyable experiences. To take that away because of not living a healthy lifestyle is irresponsible. So do yourself a favor, trade in the substances for exercise and some healthy foods. It may be a little difficult at first because some may develop some dependencies from the substances, but in the long run, your body, mind, and partner will thank you.

These issues don't affect younger men and women as much as they affect those who are slightly older, mostly because of the time in which a person has indulged in drinking and smoking. But at the end of the day, those who drink and smoke regularly have health issues. Of course, there are exceptions to this rule, just like with any and everything. But they are far in between. But why gamble with your body and mind?

Questions for Reflection:

1. What areas of your health do you need to focus on most: physical, mental, or spiritual?

2. What goals can you make today to help bring you closer to a place of holistic health?

3. How have health issues held you back from an abundant life in the past? Does that motivate you to make positive changes?

Notes

_____
_____
_____
_____
_____
_____
_____
_____
_____
_____
_____
_____
_____
_____
_____
_____
_____
_____
_____
_____
_____
_____
_____
_____
_____
_____
_____
_____

CHAPTER TWO

☙

Time

Are you using your time wisely? Are you using your time to acquire all of the things that will give you a life of abundance? Or are you using your time to only acquire one or two of the items? I'm not here to judge. I am here to give you an objective opinion of what I think wealth is. Some will use all their time acquiring material wealth and accumulating enough money to help others but won't help others because they think they don't have enough. There are some who will use their time to acquire only happiness; meanwhile, they go broke. Some will misuse their time seeking ultimate spirituality and will wait on God to drop down from the sky and hand them a million dollars. I'm saying that one must be diverse with his or her time. One must not put all his or her time eggs in one basket. Diversify your time.

James 2:20 says that *"faith without works is dead"* (NLT). Meaning that trusting in God but not putting in the work is a waste of your time. So, diversifying your time with God while putting in the proper work that is required to reach your goals and spirituality is imperative. God is not going to come down and do anything for you. He works through you. He tells you through your time that you communicate with him in prayer and meditation (both of which are very important) what He needs you to do for Him. Some of these things may be to help you; some of the things He says may be for you to help others. Both are important for reaching your goals of a life of abundance. Helping others may be more important in reaching your goals. That's a debatable subject, and we will speak more on it letter in the book.

Be careful of those who waste your time. Or those who waste your time are just as bad as those who rob you of money. You can acquire wealth again. But once time is lost, it is gone forever. Those who have no true perception of time are just as bad as those with no money. People will spend every dime they have without even understanding or knowing where it went. It's even worse for people who waste their and other people's time. They may spend every waking moment at work or every moment of life goofing off. But they have wasted so much time on one area of life they have missed the other key ingredients for their delicious meal called life. In my opinion, a person with an abundance of time and no money is just as rich as a person who has an abundance of money with no time. A person with an abundance of time with not a lot of money and understanding the other laws of living a life of abundance can have just as great a life as a person with money and no time. Time allows you the ability to carefully choreograph plans. It allows you to work on strengthening your other attributes. When using time wisely, a person can increase his physical and mental health, ultimately making him smarter. The better the blood flows through the body, the better you will be able to think, and the better you think, the more knowledge and wisdom you will be able to comprehend. The more knowledge and wisdom you will be able to comprehend, the better you will understand the knowledge of God and the Universe. This should ultimately increase your ability to be happy. This is just one scenario. The possibilities are endless when it comes to time. But just as easy as one's life could be enhanced when using his time wisely, one could destroy his life the same way. A person must keep themselves busy in a positive way if they have an abundance of time. If he or she doesn't, he or she could easily destroy themselves with the unfortunate abundance of time-wasting things that this world has to offer. The overuse of legal and illegal drugs, negative music, television, and social media are time wasters and will never lead to anything positive.

Who will be able to travel more in this scenario? You have a person with a great job. They make enough money that they are able to save for a vacation. They make $250,000 a year. Their bills are paid, and they have money to spend. They work 40 to 50 hours a week with accumulated vacation time, 10 hours a month if they don't call off or get sick. They receive a minimum of 50 hours of vacation time every year. On the other hand, we have a person who has a decent job making 25 to 30 thousand a year. Let's say their bills are paid because they have lived within their means. They work 20 hours a week and because they are less stressed because of an easier job position, they are in a healthier State of mind. The person with less can ultimately have more if he or she does what needs to be done according to God's will. He will have more time to travel, help others, spend time with his family, and if he or she wants to, they can use the time to obtain more knowledge to better their living situation.

Keep in mind that the future does not yet exist. The only thing that will ever exist is the present. If a person wants to prepare him or herself for the future, he must do what is important in the present. The so-called future will always align itself with the present.

Questions For Reflection:

4. In what ways can you better manage your time? Take a look at your priorities. List them out from highest to lowest in terms of importance. Take out some of the things at the bottom. Use that time to further your life of abundance.

5. Be honest: do you take enough time for yourself? With newfound time, what hobbies and pursuits would you invest in?

6. Do you see your time as valuable? Why or why not?

CHAPTER THREE

~

Material Things

There's a saying that says money can't buy happiness. I'm not going to go into if this is true or not, but one thing that I am sure of is that not having money can make you unhappy. When those bills begin to pile up, sadness and despair can set in quickly. When the first of the month comes around and your rent or mortgage is due, plus the utility bills, it's a little harder to smile when the stresses of life occur. So, on your journey to be happy, make sure you try to earn a good living. It'll make living a life of abundance a lot easier.

Giving

There is also the responsibility that comes with having money. Previously, we touched briefly on giving and helping others. Giving could possibly be the most important thing about having a life of abundance. It is one of the best ways to showcase how blessed and how filled with abundance your life really is. Most ancient texts, such as the Bible and other religious books, say that give and you will receive blessing from the most high. Keep in mind that God is not coming down and putting in manual labor. He works through you and me. The wages He pays us come in many forms.

Helping others is one of the best ways to showcase your life of surplus. Buying flashy things is what the average person does when he or she thinks they are ahead in life, but this book is not about being average. The only way that a person is known to have more than he needs is by giving it away.

Most of the time, when people think of giving, they think of giving money. But that's probably the least important thing we need to give others. There are many other ways to give to others. Money is a material object and can be lost if given to someone. But the gift of knowledge and happiness is even more infinite than anything. Giving knowledge can pretty much cover all of the subjects in this book which is why I chose to write it. This is my gift to you. Of course, in order to give, a person that you are giving it to must be ready to receive it. Unfortunately, there are some who just will not accept this knowledge. We're not talking about them. They are a few steps behind on this journey and need more time to catch up. Trying to tell someone something who doesn't want to hear it is a waste of time and is a turn-off to those you are talking to. That is the equivalent of walking up to someone and giving them a ham sandwich who doesn't eat ham. You're just wasting time and energy. Save your breath and give it to those who want the knowledge. There are millions of people who are ready to receive whatever it is that you have to give. Concentrate on those people and let the universe concentrate on the others, for their time is coming.

Rhetorically speaking, how rich are you that you have so much that you can give some of your abundance away? How much can you give to those who have less than you? Would you be able to help someone in need? Or would you say I need for myself and I don't have anything to give? These are questions that will be asked of you in the future, and you will have to answer. Just like living a life of abundance, some will think that giving is all about money or material things. Being able to give money is a wonderful thing. It saves you time to do other things. But just like I have stated over a dozen times in this wonderful book that you are reading, abundance is much more than that. One of the easiest ways to know that you are living a life of abundance is by how much you have to give. Some may think they don't have anything to give because they have all of the other factors except money. But money is only one factor. How about a person with less money and a lot of time. These things will be a trigger for the universe to give you the money you so desire. Giving to others is a clear sign to the universe that you have discovered that you have more than you need and that you choose to give some of your extra to others. And because of these, the universe will give you 10 times as much as you already have because that's the way the universe works. The Universal law of giving is that the Universe, AKA God or whatever your religious beliefs or culture calls Him or Her, will provide those that give the tools they need to give more to others, no matter the form. God and the universe is not a physical object. So, it does not physically give to those in need. Instead, it trusts in those who understand how the universe works to do this for it, and in return, he rewards you extremely generously. It's almost like a job. You go to work every day for a company, probably 8 to10 hours a day. After a week or two, that job gives you a check for your services. The Universe is the same way. But ask yourself this: who will pay better? A human being that may or may not like you? Or an infinite, all-knowing, loving energy that owns any and everything. So next time you say you don't have time to give and do the universe's work, ask yourself what is more important—working for others or doing the work of the most high? The answer is simple. God.

There are many creative ways to be able to give back and help others. You might be able to give your time to a homeless shelter. Going down to a homeless shelter can sometimes be challenging and taxing mentally. You might see people in situations that you never imagined. There are too many negative scenarios to mention, and the purpose of this book is to concentrate on the positive. But in the same place, you see people who may be struggling financially but are still happy. Still, they are beautiful people inside and out. Your purpose in their life may just be to give them a little motivation in the form of positive energy, a smile, or a hot cooked meal. The giving possibility is endless, and there is no one way to give in that situation.

At this point, you understand the concept of time, so you have no excuse for saying you don't have time to help others. If you think you don't have time to help others or think your situation is too bad to lend a helping hand, then you may want to stop reading this book. To reiterate, you always have time as long as you're alive. Whether you budget and use your time wisely is up to you

Another way to give is to some children who may need mentoring, or cook some food for a food bank and give out food. There are millions of ways to give. You may be a spiritual person and know a lot about God and the universe. You may have to give someone that knowledge. Because you understand that God and the universe are infinite, you feel there is no need to keep all the knowledge of the universe to yourself. So, you pass this knowledge on to others to help them on their journey. In return, the universe may reward you with other key factors for a life of abundance.

Questions for Reflection:

1. What do you think of when you think of giving? Is money the first thing that comes to your mind?

2. Consider your unique circumstances at the moment. What is the more productive way you could give at this time?

3. Think of a time when someone gave you something influential in your life, no matter what it was, material or otherwise. How did that impact you? How can you provide that same impact on someone else's life?

Notes

CHAPTER FOUR

∽

Intelligence

Knowledge and wisdom

W hat is knowledge? Depending on who you ask, you will get a few different answers. Some say knowledge is when you go to school and acquire a degree in one particular subject. Some would say true knowledge is the knowledge of self. The dictionary states that knowledge is defined as the fact or condition of knowing something with familiarity gained through experience or association. The truth of the matter is they are all correct. If a person goes to college and requires a degree, he has gained acknowledgment to have understood the knowledge of one particular subject, which is a knowledge to buy the certificate of completion. This is an amazing accomplishment and should never go unnoticed. But one should never look down or up to a person with or without a degree because that is just foolishness and jealousy. A degree is an important thing because it shows a person's ability to complete a task. It used to guarantee a person a job, but now times are a little harder than they were a few years ago. So, it may take a little more to get the dream job you want.

Those who do not have a degree should not fret, keeping in mind that most of the billionaires we know never finished college, i.e., Bill Gates, Mark Zuckerberg, and a few other notable guys. With that said, go to school, take an online class, and learn something. Because without this form of knowledge, you can't understand knowledge and wisdom as a whole. I'm not saying go and study quantum mechanics. But just learn something. This will help you exercise your mind for other things that you may want or need to use your mind for in the future. It's just like physical exercise. The more you do it, the easier it'll be. Another form of knowledge is learning from one's mistakes, or more importantly, the mistakes of others. If you see a person walk down an alley and get robbed, you should automatically gain the knowledge to know that it is a bad idea to walk down that alleyway.

Wisdom is the parent of knowledge. Wisdom can't be taught. It is learned from the continuous pursuit of knowledge.

Questions For Reflection:

1. What does wisdom mean to you?

2. How have you seen wisdom impact your life and the lives of those around you?

3. In what ways do you wish to grow in wisdom for the furtherance of a life of abundance?

Notes

CHAPTER FIVE

❧

Discipline

In order to have a life of abundance, we must have the discipline to use our time wisely. I'm not saying you must divide your time equally because it's not true. Some people are better than others in certain areas. Some may even have a head start in life, such as generational wealth or great genetics, so these people may not be able to spend as much time building wealth or working on their diet and health because it is already given to them. There is no clear formula because everyone has a different life. But one thing is for certain, without discipline, it is virtually impossible to reach all your goals.

Discipline is the ability to train or develop by instruction and exercise, especially in self-control. This means that you must have the self-control to achieve your goals. For instance, we all have time. But to use our time wisely requires discipline. It's easy to use our time to sit around and watch TV, look at social media or play video games, but we must ask ourselves, "Is this going to bring us any closer to a life of abundance?" One of the best ways is to have a schedule already set up so there is no confusion on what I should be doing at any particular time. Once again, no one can make your schedule for you because what is good for one isn't always good for another. The schedule is tailored to your liking and what you think is important at what time. You may want to set your spiritual wealth first thing in the morning. Some may want to wake up and spend an hour on themselves, relaxing and playing on social media. Remember, media and video games or whatever you like doing will still and should be done while trying to reach your goals. Making sure you are enjoying life and investing in your hobbies is an important part of true wealth because a man who spends all his time working and *no time* playing is poor, in my opinion. But ultimately, it is up to you how you want to start your day and how to end your day. Your schedule might be working on one attribute a day or spending a whole day working on one attribute (an attribute a day). The choice is up to you. As long as you are progressing and becoming more wealthy overall, you are doing great.

But ultimately, it comes back to time because, without proper time management, you can blow time doing absolutely nothing, which means just as much as a person with money and no time is poor, a person with nothing but time and no money is very poor.

It's difficult to achieve high goals without discipline. Without the discipline to pray every day, or the discipline to eat healthy every day, or the discipline to go to work every day. No matter what you have, you'll lose it.

Questions For Reflection:

1. Where can you be more disciplined in your life?

2. What goals can you make today to work on your discipline?

3. How can you see a more disciplined life shape your future? How will it make life more abundant for you?

Notes

CHAPTER SIX

❧

Freedom

L iving a life of true abundance is tricky. Some may feel they live a life of abundance because they have a large amount of one particular thing on the list. But in essence, they work so hard on receiving one or two of the things, usually wealth. But they are so far behind in the other categories. As humans, we can work so hard to be one thing or one particular category that we may subconsciously be a slave to it. An easy example is always money. Some people waste their whole life and freedom to receive wealth, but they may end up in slavery. Either slavery of their own mind, the minds of others, or in prison where they basically work for free.

Being a slave to what other people think is another example. Some of us will spend every waking moment making ourselves look a certain way to be accepted by the masses. We can go as simple as doctoring pictures to post them online or as extreme as altering our physical bodies to get more people to like or be attracted to us. This is being a slave to other people's minds. We must free ourselves of these thoughts and, most importantly, the thoughts of others to truly live a life of abundance.

Slavery comes in many forms, not just the traditional, old-fashioned 1800s slavery that some cultures may have experienced. In this new day in age, anyone can be a slave, especially Caucasians. They may be enslaved to the prison system. But most of us are slaves to money. We spend so much time and effort to get it because we think it is what is going to make us happy and successful. We spend so much time trying to receive it that once we have it, we don't know what its true value is, or we have forgotten that money is not what truly makes us wealthy. We spend more than half of our life trying to get money to live a certain way. But the truth of the matter is, we do not see the forest because the trees are in the way. For example, I had a job where I worked 5 minutes away from the water. As a man who loves fishing, every day, I would say I'm going to take a week off to go fishing. One day, being stressed from work, I had an eye-opening experience. I had to look at my life and really evaluate what was important to me. Money is very important. But it was absolutely foolish of me to not enjoy being so close to the water every day. If I couldn't make "time" to go to the water every day, even if it was just for 5 minutes, I was nothing but a slave to my job, money, and responsibilities. It doesn't take as much time and energy to be happy as it takes to build wealth. That 5 minutes that I used to spend fishing before work would recharge all of my senses and happiness for the whole day, making me seem wealthier than I was. There would have been nothing wrong with NOT going for a few minutes every day and taking a week off. But why put off till tomorrow, when you can do it today. The same rules apply to every fun thing you enjoy doing.

Some things may give us a false sense of wealth and abundance. In the new generation, some social media applications inflate one's ego to the point where they may feel as if they have more than they actually do. We must be careful and realize that the things on the computer and internet are not real. One may think that because they posted a picture on the internet and received a bunch of likes and comments from people that they never see, they are popular and have more people behind them than they really do. This will cause us to post more of our personal lives and, for some, more personal and provocative pictures in order to receive more likes for the full sense of acceptance from people on the internet. Science has shown that social media can release the same dopamine as taking hardcore drugs. The same way a person would feel after doing hardcore drugs, a person may feel after posting things on social media. Some will go as far as doctoring their picture because they are ashamed of what people will think of their true selves. If you aren't being your true self, you are a slave to what other people think of you. It is impossible to live a life of abundance if you are a slave to what other people think of you. Slavery is slavery, no matter what form it comes in. Even slavery of your own mind or the mind of others.

It's possible to have a lot of money and still not have the ability to go where you want to. We have celebrities who make millions for a single show or movie, but as soon as they walk out of their house, they are bombarded by fans. These people are prisoners of their own success. How wealthy are you if you are confined to a three-block radius of a Hollywood subdivision? A truly wealthy person who's living a life of abundance can go to a wealthy neighborhood, a poor neighborhood, a white or black neighborhood, or any other neighborhood for that matter and blend in with the natives. If you can't do this, even with having a lot of money, you have to deduct a point of how wealthy you think you are.

Questions For Reflection:

4. What does freedom mean to you?

5. In what ways have you become a slave in your life? Physically, mentally, and spiritually. Be honest with yourself and explore all of these areas.

6. What have you learned from this chapter that will help you free yourself from slavery?

Notes

CHAPTER SEVEN

～

Spirituality

We are all in need of divine power unless you are an atheist, but that's another topic. But for those who understand and believe in a supreme energy, being, or spirit, we all search for, long for that support of that which is all-seeing and all-knowing. Where I am from, we call it, Him or Her God. Depending on where you were born or what your native language is, your culture may have another name. But for all intents and purposes, let's use God. We all ask God for help and search for His wisdom. But the search for His wisdom is closer than most of us think. Stop searching for God outwardly because He is inside of you, and so is His spirit and energy. You'll never find Him until you look in the mirror. I'm not saying that you are God or that even you are a god, but that the spirit is embedded in your DNA. Due to do some different circumstances(those circumstances are not the same for every individual or group), a lot of us have lost where to find God. Some of it was lost in the translation of ancient books. Some of us lost it due to past wars or slavery. Others just lost it recently due to media, mind manipulation, or an improper diet that clogs your mind and inhibits focus. But to live a good life, there must be a balance. We must be sure to cleanse our bodies and minds of all the superfluities of life to ensure that we can access the energy of God that is inside of us and inside of others. One wrong move and the opposite of God is running you and those around you. The wrong energy will have you thinking and living foul.

Questions For Reflection:

1. What does spirituality look like in your life?

2. How can you better attune yourself with God?

3. What activities make you feel most in touch with your spiritual life? How can you make more time for these activities in your life?

Notes

CHAPTER EIGHT

☙

Happiness

The most important thing to understand about happiness is that the true essence of happiness is also already deeply rooted inside of you, in your DNA, just like God. But the difference is that it can sometimes be obtained by outside objects. But it is already in your body, your soul, spirit, and mind. Material objects and wealth can give you temporary happiness, just like when one buys a new car. That new car brings you happiness and joy. You wash it every day, clean it and make sure it looks beautiful. But just like all material objects, your love for it decreases every waking day. So, you have to get another new object. Whether it be new clothes, shoes, or another car. But when one finds happiness within themselves, they will never have to go anywhere to find it. The moment one wakes up, happiness is there. When they leave to go to work or school, the happiness is right there holding their hand. The same can be said for spirituality. Once one is truly happy, his abundance looks and feels like it will soar through the roof. A person who is genuinely happy looks and radiates true abundance. Here's a quick story: one year, while searching for my true happiness, I took some "time" off work. I wanted to use my "time" more for myself. During this period, I spent a lot of time fishing and being one with nature. While at the shore, I was kicking back with the local fishermen who were just like me; some were avid fishermen and were at the shores enough that we were on a first-name basis. Some would come down after work. Some were retired factory workers. One day, we were all sitting back barbecuing, and the guy who was barbecuing in my eyes was so wealthy because he was always the one who was giving away his fishing equipment, cooking with his food and charcoal and grill, and was one of the happiest people there. There was another guy who was a cool guy as well, but he was not as happy as the guy who usually brought the food to the barbecue. The guy who consistently barbecued, in my eyes, was a very rich and wealthy man, while the other guy who was cool but wasn't as happy seemed to struggle in life. It turns out that the unhappier guy owned a nearby factory and was financially wealthy, while the guy who threw the barbecues and brought the food every day was actually homeless. This blew my mind and was a very awakening moment for me. Here I was fishing with guys, one who was possibly a millionaire on one side of me, and on the left side of me, a homeless man who was more giving and, to the naked eye, seemed to have more than everyone there. This was when I realized how important time and giving were. I also realized that happiness is not derived from material things but mostly from within us.

No one will be happy all the time. You will always experience ups and downs. These changes are just facts of life. Everything will go up and down. Happiness, faith, money, and time. But understanding that there is more than just one factor in a life of abundance will keep you realizing that you can always have a life of abundance. There is no way that all these factors will be seen in a negative light in your mind all at the same time. This is what makes this principle so great. Even if you lose your job, you have now just acquired unlimited time. Time is always worth more than money if used correctly, so you should be able to find creative things to ensure the increase of the other factors to create a life of abundance. Working on all the other factors ensures that if you lack in an area or two, you will be prepared for the rewards of understanding that all things change on the upswing.

In my opinion, the one with the most happiness is the wealthiest. Happiness is a sign that you have completed your universe. Just like money, some people have the ability to acquire more of it with little effort. Some have to try harder to achieve ultimate happiness. But at the end of the day, it is abundant energy. Any and everyone can get any amount of it if he or she seeks it. Due to the food quality that we now have, some of us may require a little help in retrieving happiness due to chemical imbalances and such. I am no doctor, so, of course, I can't recommend or tell you when or when not to take medicine to even you out chemically. I'm going to leave that to the professionals. One thing I can tell you is that eating a healthy diet will greatly increase your chances of evening out your natural body chemicals that could lower your body's need for medicinal help. A healthy body equals a healthy mind, and a healthy mind greatly increases happiness.

A sense of humor is something everyone knows that a woman loves a man with one. And vice versa.

Questions for Reflection:

1. What does happiness look like to you?

2. What activities bring you the most happiness in your life? How can you make time to explore those activities further?

3. What aspects of your life do you need to get in order to start living a life of true happiness today?

Notes

_____

_____

_____

_____

_____

_____

_____

_____

_____

_____

_____

_____

_____

_____

_____

_____

_____

_____

_____

_____

_____

_____

_____

_____

_____

_____

CHAPTER NINE

~

Positive Thinking

L et's talk about positive thinking. Follow the path of least resistance. Back when I was in college for electrical engineering, one of their most important laws that we learned about electricity is that it always follows the path of least resistance. Let's convert that to ourselves. When going through life, there will always be obstacles and there will always be trials and tribulations. But at the end of the day, you will always reach your goals faster if you follow the path of least resistance that leads to the path of your goals.

Affirmation: You must tell yourself that you deserve a life of abundance every day. Look yourself in the mirror and mean it. The universe will heal you, and your world will begin to align with the abundance of God. But be careful because you might receive it and not even know it because you're too busy searching for just one of the things when you have everything you've already ever wanted in life.

Positive thinking. (Thinking negatively will keep you poor mentally.)

Gratitude. In order to have a life of abundance, an especially important lesson to understand is that you already have a life of abundance. You already have everything you ever wanted and needed. You must understand this concept in order for you truly live a life of abundance. Everything in the universe is already yours. It's inside of you. Happiness, wealth, time, spirituality, etc. These things are already in your hands. You hold the key to unlocking the time to utilize all of what you have already been given by God. It's up to you to understand that you already have everything. But once you understand, you must have gratitude and be thankful for what you have. Only then will the universe bring you more of what you already have. There's no way you don't have time. Time is everywhere. You must be thankful for having time. The more thankful you are, the more the universe will bring you of what you already have because you know how to properly utilize it and use it to help others.

Be Positive

The thing about life is that there are always two ways to look at it. The same people who live a life of abundance can just as easily look at their lives as living in lack. However, they choose to look at their lives is what their lives would be. It is crucial to exercise looking at life in a positive light. The more positive you look at life, the more positive life will become. We all have a life of abundance already, whether you know it or not. Sometimes we have the wrong people around us. We've watched the news, which is full of negative information about our neighborhoods, nation, and president, and we begin to look at life in a negative way. It is essential to get rid of all negative energies and spirits in every form, whether that energy is in the physical form of a person, the media, or the material form, as in drinking too much alcohol. Just a reminder that alcohol is called spirits for a reason. Giving the right condition can change your spirit from good to bad. Having negative energies and spirits around you will darken your view of life and have you think that you live a life of lack when you really are in a life of abundance. This thing can go to the millionaire with everything or the young guy in the hood. Neither one of these two people can have more than the other because it depends on the mainframe. The millionaire with everything can be unhappy, which immediately knocks him down a level in the life of abundance. The guy from the hood with happiness, time, and spirituality will have more than the millionaire and can hold his head up high. He will be able to do ten times as much on this Earth as the other person.

Questions For Reflection:

1. Do you tend to be a positive or negative person?

2. How does your answer to the previous question affect your life for better or worse?

3. If you generally tend to think negatively, what steps can you take to change your mindset to one of positivity and gratitude?

Notes

EPILOGUE/CONCLUSION

～

A life of abundance is waiting for you today. All you must do is take hold of it. If you are not currently living a life of abundance, you are the only one holding yourself back. God has already provided you with everything you will ever need. All you require is to find the motivation within yourself to take hold of it and make life everything it can be.

In today's times, life can often feel out of control. I'm begging you to not let that feeling overwhelm your mindset. That feeling is a deception and a lie! You ARE in control, whether you feel like it or not. You can crush every goal that you make for yourself. You can be healthy, happy, successful, and wealthy in every way. You have unlimited untapped potential just waiting to be drawn out. Don't let that potential sit and rot any longer. The world needs the things only you can provide. You will never know how powerfully you can impact the world until you try.

Foster a holistic view of health. Never put a limit on your dreams. Work until you've reached your goals, but also take time to recharge, rest, and engage with your hobbies. Your mind, body, and spirit are the most valuable assets you possess. Take care of them in every way, or you ultimately won't be successful in creating abundance in your life.

We weren't created to live stagnant lives with no growth. God never intended for us to be isolated, unhappy, and crushed beneath a mountain of responsibilities. God created us to thrive in the abundance of joy, health, and love. There is a different way to see the world, and there is a different way to live. Nothing is stopping you. A lifestyle of abundance is what you were made for.

Are you ready to start living your life of abundance? Embark on your grand adventure today.